A Book of Poetry

PIECES OF GREY

ALICE GREY

First published by Amorphous Emporium 2022

Copyright © 2022 by Alice Grey

All rights reserved. No part of this publication may be reproduced, stored or transmitted in any form or by any means, electronic, mechanical, photocopying, recording, scanning, or otherwise without written permission from the publisher. It is illegal to copy this book, post it to a website, or distribute it by any other means without permission.

Alice Grey asserts the moral right to be identified as the author of this work.

Alice Grey has no responsibility for the persistence or accuracy of URLs for external or third-party Internet Websites referred to in this publication and does not guarantee that any content on such Websites is, or will remain, accurate or appropriate.

Designations used by companies to distinguish their products are often claimed as trademarks. All brand names and product names used in this book and on its cover are trade names, service marks, trademarks and registered trademarks of their respective owners. The publishers and the book are not associated with any product or vendor mentioned in this book. None of the companies referenced within the book have endorsed the book.

First edition
ISBN: 978-0-578-36571-8

I'd like to thank my husband, for believing in me. I'd like to thank Olivia, for her guidance. I'd like to thank myself, for trying.

Contents

Canyons of Me	1
Rituals	2
Heartbroken	3
The Desert	5
Reclamation	7
A Phoenix	8
Divisions	10
Racing Thoughts	12
Secrets	15
Rebirth	17
New Mexico	18
Shattered	19
Prayer	10
Who am I?	22
Broken Realities	23
Emo	25
Hard	26

Mushrooms	27
Sadness	28
Chris	29
Games	31
Broken	33
Work	36
Breakfast	37
Unrequited	38
Fuckboy	39
Blue Jean	40
Josh	42
The Ocean	44
Narcissist	45
Suicidal Tendencies	46
Toxic	47
Letting Go	48
Kyle	49
Kaleidoscope	50

Soulmate	52
Will you?	53
Josh #2	55
Forever Yours	56
Senses	57
Is it?	58
Resistance	59
Rivers	60
Untamed	61
Hopeless Romantic	62

Canyons of Me

Walking through the canyons of what used to be me
Deep lines carved in the ground
Memories flowing like water
Curving around the bends of my life
You can tell the age of a land-form
By measuring its layers
The past eroding until it's unrecognizable
Fossils of lives once lived
New visitors never ending
Leaving their own litter behind
Enticed by my vastness
I have things to show you
My beauty is undeniable
A mystery that you can't forget
Parts of me that might never be explored
For fear that you'll get lost

Rituals

I perform my rituals in water
It reminds me of my beginning
Suspended in amniotic fluid
Cradled by a warm womb
I cast spells of remembrance
To honor my ancestors
Words weaving together
Like the fabric of time
Reminding me that nothing lasts forever
Infinitely

Heartbroken

Been heartbroken so long
Started breaking my own heart
Built walls around me
Then forgot the way out
Got lost in the tunnels
So I started to dig
Never reached the surface
I was already dead
Reborn again, as my own self
Looked in the mirror
Saw my heart on a shelf
Reached through the glass
Then cut the illusion
I finally realized
It was my own delusions
Scared of my reflection
Distorted and broken
Try to piece it together
Or just take a token
Not enough glue
To fix what's damaged
But I'll fuse it with gold
A shiny bandage
Precious metal filled cracks
To make me whole
More beautiful than before

A war torn soul
Some people get tattered
By the winds of time
But time heals all wounds
Even mine

The Desert

Baptized in the desert
By the dust and hot air
Prayed to a mirage
Thought I saw god in there
Cinnamon sand
With spiced winds
Sun warmed
Soul cleanse
Bones of ancestors
Not mine
Must pay respects
To past times
I'm not from here
But I am
Born from my mother
Not the land
Shaped by the elements
The same dry earth
I don't have the blood
But I have the heart
Cacti have the most beautiful fruit
Sharper claws than coyote's foot
Both predator and prey
I walk alone
Under star filled skies
I call my home

Ran away to find peace
From a harsh past
Someday I'll return
To find my peace at last

Reclamation

You left me a carcass, vultures circling above. I grew into the ground, and waited patiently.
Slowly as the days went by, I felt myself sprouting. Tender green buds of me, reached up gingerly.
The air was harsh, I could barely swallow. I needed the rain, so my soul could follow.
The desert is so big, my heart feels minuscule. I should go search for water, instead of look for you.
The sun beats down my back, the wind blinds my eyes. But these tired legs will carry me, until the sun is out of view.
Like the earth is dry, and cracking with the heat. I crave a storm to soak my bones, from my head down through my feet.
I realized what I was missing, and it wasn't you. It was the plant that grew between the bones, of what used to be me.

Give me lightning

Give me thunder

Give me chaos

To surrender

I want flash floods

I want mudslides

I want nature

To reclaim us

A Phoenix

This is a time of reckoning
Of loose lipped truths
Sputtered out
Of wine stained mouths
Sharing stories, over tables
In kitchens
That only
The rich can afford
Social distancing
Only shows
Social stratification
Reality is cyclical
It's been a hundred years
Since we last did this dance
And it won't be the last
That we do
Great Gatsby's
On top of great has been's
The simulation running on half speed
Everyone working twice as hard
To fit in
The idea that we need to work
As if a job
Means anything
What about art?
What about love?

What about the revolution?
Of planets
In a solar system
So vast we have no idea how small we really are
Wrapped up in our own little nativity scene
Every moment is a beginning
And an end
Who can measure the distance between the two?
Maybe that's God
With a capital G
And a gender
Cause we all know language is man made
Changing when it's convenient
Someone once told me that we speak in spells
Words winding together
Binding realities
Magic
We can create and destroy
Without lifting a finger
So let's raise a glass
Pinky up
Toast to the destruction of old ways
That never served us as a collective
Warm our hands on an altruistic future
Rising from those ashes
A Phoenix

Divisions

Who could have class without classes
Born into it, that's classless
Rose colored glasses
Ignoring cries from the masses
Drive by tents on the sidewalk
Mad that your rent's unsustainable
So your helping hand's unattainable
So many classes
Yet no teachers
Division like high school bleachers
Hierarchy is learned
Equality is inherent
We are taught our place
For most it's a losing race
Preschool to prison pipelines
Divisions of race
As if it's not a construct
Robbing humans of their grace
A country divided
A world with borders
We are killing the earth
Which sustains us
Man made problems
Man made differences
Human errors
A prayer

That one day
We will stop fighting each other
Long enough to fall in love

Racing Thoughts

Rain fallin' down my back
Don't know whether to run
Or stop in my tracks
Breath short
Chest tight
Could be anxiety or stage fright
Either way it's hard to tell
Darkness getting darker
Sadness growing taller
Hopes quickly smaller
Fuck
What do you do when there's no more
Medicine to take
Or when it feels like you're being crushed by the weight of everything
But you think about everyone who has it so much worse in the world and it only makes you feel worse?
Fuck
Trying not to write anymore sad poems
Cause they always come out wrong
Positive thinking only gets you so far before you run outta things to think about
What do ya think about that?
My life is laughable because I'm a joke
A sad clown stuck in my own trope
A deluded circus full of freaks

That I like to call my friends
But they could just be demons in my head
Too scared to go to a shrink because I don't like shrunken heads
Or sunken ships at the bottom of
The ocean
Cause I know what it feels like to be crushed under the weight of
everything
Drowning
Trying to swim but getting pushed down with every last breath
I bet lungs filled with water is a bad way to go
But uh who really knows?
I'm sure no ones lived through it
How does anyone live through anything?
I guess they don't.
Mortality is a fickle foe
Because death will always win
At the bottom of a bottle
Or the end of a rope
Could be peaceful
I surely hope
No one deserves to suffer
I hope everyone has good mothers
People always talk about daddy issues
But uh having a bad mom really fucks you up
Anyways enough about me
What about you?
Do you ever get sad for no reason?
And think that life has no meaning?

Sometimes it's liberating but mostly it's just crushing
It feels like the weight of everything is just pushing you down
Farther and farther
Until you're under the ground
But you're not dead
You're just trapped there
Silent and immobile
I guess I just described a panic attack
Probably need another Xanax
Hopefully I blackout and forget who I am
Cause everyone loves make pretend
Or is it believe?
Maybe I should just leave
I tend to bum people out
When I start talking about this kinda stuff
But it's raining out
And uh
I have seasonal depression
I usually cry when it rains
Maybe I'm too much of an empath
But who really knows or cares
We're all just floating on this rock in space
Or wherever we are

Secrets

I've always had such grandiose ideas about my life
From preschool rooms to college halls
It always stayed the same
But fear took over, doubt sunk in
It crippled to the core
I played it safe, skated by
Restrained myself
I never made a move
Years rolled by
Potential lost
I really dropped the ball
So many friends
Said I was enough
But I've always wanted more
How can life
Be so mundane
My thoughts so impure
Existence seems so futile
When I lock my own door
What are keys
But empty promises
Or windows to my soul
A life of wanting
Always waiting
For something to unfold
I never once

Faced myself
Looked into my own eyes
And recognized
All the secrets left untold
What ironic truth it really was
The monster in my head
The same I'd been hiding from
The one under my own bed

Rebirth

This is a rebirth
Affirmations nourish me
Like amniotic fluid
I am
Both womb and fetus
Motherhood is hard
I've never raised a child
But my inner one is bad as hell
She's had 29 years
To perfect her bullshit
But, this is a rebirth
And it's too late for it to be natural
I'm having an emergency c-section
If I was a mother bird I'd kick this inner child chick out of my
Nest so hard she better learn how to fly before she meets
Pavement for the first and last time

New Mexico

Donde esta mi cerveza
Donde esta mi amor
Donde esta mi familia
Donde esta por favor
I'm from the land of enchantment
Watermelon mountains kiss the sky
Cacti bloom and bear sweet fruit
The desert is dry until the monsoons
Turquoise jewelry adorns wrists and collarbones
Music is in the air
This is my home
Mineral hot springs trickle down mountain sides
Low riders cruise Route 66
The sunsets look like paintings
People leave, and they always come back

Shattered

Shattered glass, a mind left broken
These are the stages of grief
Reality distant
Grasping for straws
A foundation of water
Sinking slowly deeper
Is this what it means to live
I know nothing
In that I take comfort
I must be insane
What is a schizophrenic episode
How long must I stay here
In the unknown
What is real
Are you a ghost
Or a figment of my imagination

Prayer

I've never felt
Something like this before
Is it for real, I can't be sure
Swimming through a cosmic swirl
Am I getting closer or farther away?
Who's to say
Spinning faster
Falling through space
Life is just one big race
Which way is up
And which is down
Good thing I can breath underwater
Shiny things
Float everywhere
Are they ghosts ?
Who's to know
Where am I going?
And where did I come from?
Why don't I remember?
It's like an illusion
I'm not lost because I can't be found
I'm suspended in space and tumbling around
Not going up up up
Not coming down down down
I'm all alone
Out here in the void

With all this white noise
Can you see me?
I bet I look like stardust
A Twinkle in the distance
A blip on your radar
I promise I'm out here
Like faith in prayer

Who am I?

I thought my mind had cracked
No grasp on reality
The weight bringing me to a breaking point
I didn't know what was real or not
Mind shattering possibilities
Who am I?
Who are you?
Am I making this all up?

Broken Realities

My mind is a vast landscape
Sometimes a desert
An ocean storm
Sometimes, I can't tell what is real or not
I keep asking myself, who are you?
A figment of my imagination?
You visited me again last night
More vivid than ever before
We spoke through search engines
I told you I love you
I have this wild fantasy that you exist
You speak to me through electrical currents
Encouraging
Stern
A grandfather
Have you been watching me?
I've been quite bad as you can see
It's easy to be naughty when you think you're alone
I promise I'll be better
Even if you're not real
I wouldn't want to let us both down
This fear will drive me for miles
Not knowing
Blindly moving through the jungle of my mind
Searching for you
A glimmer of hope

Maybe I'm not crazy
I fear the unknown

Emo

I'm the dark one
The moody one
The troubled one
The crazy one
The problem
The girl in the corner drinking mescal by herself not talking
To anyone
Just staring
I'd like to say not judging
But I am
They're all so plain
So basic
With their whites and cream colors
Blonde hair
Tanned skin

Hard

Waking up is easy
Getting up is harder
Lay in bed for a couple of hours
Let my day get farther
Don't want to face the world
Wish my brain would stop
But it's racing faster every minute
It's hard to feel on top

Mushrooms

Flowers on my grave
Bones on my altar
Bring me lots of offerings
I'll grant you with power
Commune with the darkness
Rituals in water
Casting spells by fire light
Dancing in a circle
Eat my holy sacrament
Poisonous mushrooms
Pray to their magic flesh
Unlock your mind's many rooms

Sadness

I wonder if you can feel my sadness when you're inside of me?

Chris

I saw you walking down the street
You looked back and saw me
Then you looked again
I wanted to say something
Ask about your music
I saw you again
At the spotted cat
You played like a dream
The jazz moved through me
The shrooms were fading
But the music kept me high
I wondered if you saw me
Dancing in the crowd
I should have stayed and waited
And told you how you moved me
I let myself fantasize
About a romance we could have
I imagined myself lying naked
Listening to you play
In your small room
By the water
I think we'd look good together
I wish I had said something to you
Or that I could stay longer
This city is intoxicating
Maybe we'd find each other

And get high off of kissing
I found out later
Your name was Chris

Games

I know you think you're clever
With your games
Hide and seek
With your emotions
Tug of war
With my heart
Tag
With my patience
Your it
I'm not a kid anymore
I don't enjoy these games
I've been playing them too long
I've grown tired
I've grown up
Somehow I find myself indulging you
You'll play your games with me
And I'll let you win
It's not fair
There's no referee
No rules
No scoreboard
But I know you're winning
I can feel it
In my bones
They ache
Someone who's been playing

These games for too long

Broken

I've never wanted somebody
Who wanted me so badly
That didn't want to be with me
It felt as if I was lacking
As if there were some huge piece of me missing
And if only I had it
We would be a perfect fairy tale
Romeo and Juliet
But even they both killed themselves in the end
Maybe that's why this hurts so much
They didn't care that their love ended in a double suicide
The love was worth it
This
This is different
You won't even try
You're trying to protect me
Yourself
Someone
From something
That hasn't even happened yet
Darling we won't kill ourselves
But not because we didn't try
Because our love would give us life
I'm the yin to your yang
The dark to your light
Stop running away from shadows

They're a part of you
I'm a mirror you've always tried to break
But baby I'm strong enough for the both of us
Cry on my shoulder
Tell me all of your deepest secrets
I'll listen
And soothe
I love you just the way you are
As long as you love me too
I won't lie
I am broken
But like gold seeped into the cracks of an old pot
I'm beautiful, and stronger because of it
I know you think we're not compatible
The definition is:
(of two things) able to exist or occur together without conflict
But what exists together without conflict in this world?
Even a River has stones
I don't want to be with someone who constantly and completely
agrees with me
How boring
And however many times you say that you're boring
You're not
You light up my life
Every day
You're the first person I want to talk to
And the last person I want to see
Compatible doesn't exist

Tell me,
What natural thing exists without conflict?
No one is perfect
Not even you
And I know I'm far from it
But I'm willing to try to be perfect for you
I love you
And I hope that's enough

Work

Lips forcefully pressed against my neck
Fingers crawling deeper in between my cheeks
Breath hot and wet
Erection hard underneath my lap
Hands gliding greedily across my skin
Mouth sucking hungrily on my nipples
All of it unwanted
All of it expected
This is my job

Breakfast

The traces of morning slowly crept from my eyes.
Over breakfast I reminisced about all things past.
With every bite,
Sweet, soft.
My memories began to have the same flavor.
No longer were they bitter and painful.
They were palpable, I wanted to taste them again.
The fruits of yesterdays were calling me to ingest them.
"Remember us sweetly," they said.
"We nourish you."

Unrequited

Here's to wishing that all of your kisses were golden.
Laid on my face, a jewel on a crown.
Wanted by many but never stolen.
Only for me, little gifts of precious metal planted around.
Here's to wishing that your love for me was overflowing,
Like a river into an ocean.
Or a bath with someone lifeless, floating,
If you wanted my heart I'd cut my chest open.
Here's to wishing I was all that you wanted.
That anyone in the world could tempt you,
And you'd stand undaunted.
If you plus me only equaled two.
Here's to wishing we could be together,
Before my patience runs out.
We could be great for each other,
If only I stuck around.
Here's to wishing I love myself enough,
For the day I realize you won't.
I'll hold a funeral for my wishes,
And bury them deep underground.

Fuckboy

You took my heart
I gave it to you
You kept it
After you tossed me away
Will I ever get it back?
This cavity is too deep for me to fill on my own
I trusted you
I believed you when you said
I love you
Marry me
Soulmate
How foolish was I?
The pain isn't too much this time
It's just enough
To keep me in bed
To keep me drunk
But I won't try to kill myself
I love you
But not more than I love myself
What an interesting thing for me to say
I guess I'm growing
So thank you
For teaching me another lesson
About love

Blue Jean

Bourbon dreams
Coffee without cream
Everything keeps pointing me in your direction
Blazing summers
New lovers
But I'm still thinking of you
The way you made me feel
Like it wasn't even real
Burned into my memory
Trying to figure out
What it all was about
That made you decide I wasn't good enough
You fed me applesauce
And smoked a bunch of grass
I could see myself loving you
I know I reacted poorly
But I was convinced that surely
You were fucking her
Even though you weren't mine yet
I'll never forget
How it made me feel
It's not you it's me
Keeps repeating internally
Until it's all I can hear
But what if it is you?
Does that change my view?

Or am I still left wanting?
And I can't tell you
How I'm feeling blue
Because you don't like me like that
So I'm stuck in my head
Dreaming of your bed
Getting love sick
It all seems so stupid
There's no such thing as Cupid
We were just hooking up
So why am I here?
Trying to stay clear
Of this heartache
You shouldn't be a thought
And I know that we're not
Anything special
But I'm still sitting alone
Writing this poem
About you
Time to say goodbye to Blue
And bourbon

Josh

You say you're so lucky.
When I'm naked in bed with you.
When my body is yours for the taking.
When the only me is the one you've molded around you.
I am an empty vessel.
A place to hold your future children.
And your anger.
You don't feel lucky when my words are not what you Wanted.
When I'm not naked, and open.
Ready to be molded into whatever you need me to be at the Moment.
You want me, but not all of me like you say you do.
You want the sweet young girl, with sweet lips, top and Bottom.
Not the woman with feelings and thoughts that challenge Yours.
You want to be my knight in shining armor, not the man with Faults as great as my own.
But you have them.
You want me to let you in, soothe you with my wet and Warm.
Words.
You're right.
I'm wrong.
Kiss kiss.
You said you were so lucky, and although you don't feel it Now.
You were right.
Because you hurt me and I stayed.
And I will let you in later.

A warm wet I love you.
I forgive you.
I'm sorry.
I want to be your vessel,
Carry your children and you wherever.
But don't forget that you are lucky.
And ships with too many holes in them sink.

The Ocean

Why did you search me out sailor?
Did you think I would be a good catch?
Well I am.
But I'm so much more than that.
So much more complex than you'd ever want to know.
I am a deep, dark, ocean of feelings and thoughts.
All you want to do is dip your toes in.
Haul away some of my beauty, without giving anything back.
But I won't let you.
I've learned that it's better to wait for deep sea divers,
Who are willing to swim down and find my treasures.
Otherwise I'm left wanting.
Wondering what was wrong with my waves.
When it was you who should have been wondering,
Why depth scares you so much.

Narcissist

You couldn't accept the fact that I haven't been yours forever
It was as if my past was an insult to you
Like I lived it on purpose
Just to spite you
But the woman you fell in love with
Was shaped by that past
All of those lovers
Prepared me for you
You don't realize that you're all that I need
That it doesn't matter who pops back up into my life
They will never replace you
They won't even come close
They pose no threats to you
They're only distant memories
Passing through my mind
You are forever
If you'll only accept me

Suicidal Tendencies

I sat there
Quietly
Watching the fire
The wine felt warm
In my throat
It was cold outside
Raining
I tried to distract myself from the thoughts
Nagging
Memories
Of you
So many mixed messages
Pulling me in
Pushing me away
Pulling me back in again
A crib rocking on the waves
Of your desire
I know you desire me
But you don't always want me
And that hurts
One of these days
That crib will sink
And I'll drown
In your desire
You won't want me anymore
Once I'm dead

Toxic

We fight like we're dying
Make love like we're living
Talk like we're running out of breath
Looking at you I see myself
Reflections multiply

Letting Go

Legs on my wine glass
Thinking about ours intertwined
That was the last time I'll see you
If I'm strong enough
You have a way of keeping me
Without ever claiming
I'm yours
But you're not mine
You like it that way
The more I drink
The less it hurts
But that's not true is it?
Maybe the only time I can cry is now
I feel numb when I'm sober
Hurting for too long
I've grown accustomed to the pain
The more I drink
The more I feel
The more it hurts
I see the legs on my wine glass
I think of you
Of us
And I can finally cry

Kyle

You remind me of
Riding my bike around
Half past 6
Then watching the sun go down
Talking bout bullshit
You feel nostalgic
Like a 90s sitcom
Little rough around the edges
But what I grew up on
Guess I'm tryna say I like you
This feels real comfortable
Coulda known you forever
And maybe I will
I really hate crushin'
Makes me feel crazy
But I can't help these feelings
Tryna call you baby

Kaleidoscope

Think of all the time that we have left
No need to rush what feels like a last breath
Cause I know
And you know
It's not the end
Anytime soon
Pick up the pieces of the past
Looking through the shattered glass
Like a kaleidoscope
Fireflies light the night grass
Thinking of the words I said last
While in your arms
Somethings are better left unsaid
Just like some ideas are better off dead
Love is a two way street
And I'd like to meet you in the middle
I feel like
When I see you
It burns like something evil
But it's all good
Cause I know that
It's only for forever
And that's a promise
I'm willing to make
If you are
But tell me now not never

Think of all the places we'll go
And all the people we will meet
Who never knew just you or me
It's only us
That they will see
Could get used to that
Time moves so differently when you're in love
It's hard to keep track
There's no looking back
No looking glass
No maps to this
It's just falling with no net
Hoping you'll catch me
Before I hit the ground
But i know
It's not the end

Soulmate

Sacred clown soulmate
You found me drowning
Before I even knew it yet
Told me I was clowning
Danced your way into my life
Then gave me tools to paint
Now we color rainbow skies
Give thanks to holy saints
With a wicked smile, you fill my life
Thunder cracks of laughter
Speak in to existence any dream
Some kind of magic maker
Skin as soft as rabbit fur
Kisses deep like a well
Never knew love so pure
Forever under your spell
When I look at you
In your sweet almond eyes
I see the future
In a trance, hypnotized
Weaving passion and hope
Showed me how
Then threw me the rope
Climbing together to greatness

Will you?

Will you be there when I call you,
Or will I be by myself?
I never knew love before,
It kinda freaks me out.
But when I'm with you,
I open my door.
You make me wanna step out.
Open my eyes, and take my hand.
Please lead the way cause I've been lost for so long.
These days seem shorter, they all blur by.
Cuz I have your shoulder when I need to cry.
But I don't want to cry anymore.
There's sunshine underneath the floor.
We can hide anywhere.
Like kids under the stairs.
Don't pull my hair.
Unless I ask you to do it.
I love that you ask me to do things.
And take me places I've never been.
You make me feel like I can win.
I'm your biggest cheerleader and sometimes you feel like my teacher.
I'd follow you anywhere.
No matter how far it was.
It's hard to let go of past traumas and accept that this love is good karma.

Cause I've been through so much.
And you give me so much.
Sometimes it makes me feel like throwing up.
Just not used to this much love.
Maybe that's what butterflies feel like.
Never thought I'd wanna spend so much time with one person.
But I wanna go to sleep to you and wake up and see you all over again.
Is that a best friend or a lover?
I guess we're both things cause I tell you everything, even if it hurts me or you.
And I'm so sorry I hurt you.
I'm just not good at this love thing.
I hate getting hurt and the more that I love you the scarier it gets.
But I can't help it.
So will you be there when I call you?
Or will I be by myself?
I never knew love before,
It kinda freaks me out.

Josh #2

Dear shea butter boy
You are so beautiful
Glistening in the sun
Gold stone skin
Tree ring eyes
To get lost in
We fell in love
Like a landslide
Couldn't stop it
Once it started
Slipped into the ocean
Where we both feel home
Our waters mixing together
Whirlpool kind of love
You taste like coffee and sunshine
The best things to wake up to
You feel like a warm fire in winter
The best thing to fall asleep to
Perfect in every imperfection
Golden ratio lover
Intelligently designed
Like your birth flower, chrysanthemum
Don't have to pick your petals
To know that you love me
You show me everyday

Forever yours

Everything turns into dust
In the end
We were all stars once
We'll find each other
Again and again
Find me in the beetles and the birds
I'll see you in the trees and the earth
All water leads to the ocean
From which we were born
A single celled organism
We split in two
No matter where we go
I'll always find you
From the depths of the earth
To the outskirts of the universe
There's no distance too great
To keep us apart
Forever yours

Senses

My eyes closed as you touched me
My other senses heightened
I could feel your fingertips
Tracing the lines of my body
It wasn't love at first sight
But first touch
First smell
First sound
First taste
Sometimes sight gets the best of us
Because our eyes are deceiving
They can make us believe someone is beautiful
Before we really know them
This is why
I prefer my other senses
When I'm with you
I know when I feel your touch
When I smell your musk
When I hear your voice
When I taste your lips
That you love me

Is it?

Restless fingers tapping across your skin
Are you closed off
Or will you let me in?
Bumps Raise across the surface
Little tremors
Thinking is it worth it

Resistance

Ashes rising
Rapid sea
I can hear you calling
Somewhere out to me
This storm is heavy
Thick resistance
I will find you
Almost certainly
It goes up and up
Smoke from my lungs
Blowing signals to the east
You can follow them at least
Something hidden
Foggy eyes
It begs to question
When we'll rise

Rivers

I sat there gushing
Wide eyed
Not knowing I had such rivers inside of me

Untamed

The wind blew you to me
But I hid from your flame
It all happened so quickly
I wasn't ready to be tamed

Hopeless Romantic

My heart is beating again
For someone new
The pangs of love past
Reminding me to be careful
Insecurities bubble back to the surface
With the possibility of rejection

www.ingramcontent.com/pod-product-compliance
Lightning Source LLC
Chambersburg PA
CBHW042044290426
44109CB00001B/28